What Color Is Your Parachute?
JOB-HUNTER'S WORKBOOK

Copyright © 2010 by Richard N. Bolles

All rights reserved.
Published in the United States by Ten Speed Press, an imprint of the
Crown Publishing Group, a division of Random House, Inc., New York.
www.crownpublishing.com
www.tenspeed.com

Ten Speed Press and the Ten Speed Press colophon are registered trademarks
of Random House, Inc.

Previous editions of this work were published in 1998 and 2005 by Ten Speed Press,
Berkeley, CA.

Library of Congress Cataloging-in-Publication Data
Bolles, Richard Nelson.
   What color is your parachute? job-hunter's workbook : how to create a
picture of your ideal job or next career / by Richard N. Bolles. — 3rd ed.
      p. cm.
   Summary: "The new edition of this companion workbook to *What Color Is
Your Parachute?* helps job-hunters create a picture of their ideal job or
next career"—Provided by publisher.
 1. Job hunting. 2. Vocational guidance. 3. Career changes. I.
Title. II. Title: Job-hunter's workbook.
  HF5382.7.B643 2010
  650.14—dc22
                                        2010036328
 ISBN 978-1-58008-009-5

Printed in the United States of America

Design by Colleen Cain

10 9 8 7 6 5 4 3 2

Third Edition

WHAT COLOR IS YOUR PARACHUTE?
JOB-HUNTER'S WORKBOOK

THIRD EDITION

"How to Create a Picture of Your Ideal Job or Next Career"

by Richard N. Bolles

TEN SPEED PRESS
Berkeley

Preface

Why a workbook for job-hunters and career-changers? Wouldn't a job application form be more to the point?

Nope. It wouldn't be. U.S. government statistics reveal that even in the most difficult of times at least three million people find jobs each month, and yet another two million vacancies remain unfilled. So, there are jobs out there, and millions are finding them. What is the secret of these successful job-hunters? Well, three things:

1. **They work smarter.** They know what job-hunting methods work best, and they invest their time wisely as a result. Highest among successful job-hunting methods is Beginning Your Job Hunt by Inventorying Yourself.

2. **They work harder.** They are willing to put in the time necessary to find appropriate careers and appropriate job-openings. They don't expect someone else—the government, private agencies, or other parts of "officialdom"—to do the job for them. They are willing to take the time to do a detailed inventory of who they are, doing some hard thinking, as in this *Workbook*.

3. **They work longer.** Once they have a detailed inventory of who they are, they go out looking for a job that matches *that*. In hard times or in a period coming out of hard times, it often takes far longer to find a job than most job-hunters anticipate. *Successful job-hunters or career-changers* can keep at it for many months, if necessary, because they have the energy. That energy is born of enthusiasm—they have defined a job they would just die to do, and they are determined to find it, or something as close to it as possible.

This is in contrast to job-hunters who don't take the time or trouble to figure out what work they would most delight to do, and therefore plod through their job-hunt, easily tired, easily discouraged, looking for a job that leaves them uninspired.

What Color Is Your Parachute? Job-Hunter's Workbook is therefore your key to greatly increasing your chances of finding work, provided you're willing to work smarter, work harder, and work longer than most job-hunters. The author is Dick Bolles, more formally known as Richard N. Bolles, author of the most successful job-hunting book in history—with ten million copies sold to date, and used in twenty-six countries around the world. This *Workbook* is a companion to that classic job-search guide, *What Color Is Your Parachute?* (revised and updated annually).

This full-color *Job-Hunter's Workbook* (also revised), with its user-friendly exercises and simple step-by-step worksheets, will illuminate your favorite transferable skills, fields of knowledge, people-environments, working conditions, levels of responsibility and salary, values, and goals. Once you've completed the workbook, you'll have a comprehensive picture of your dream job, and be able to pursue it with hope.

The Flower Exercise
A PICTURE OF THE JOB OF YOUR DREAMS

In order to hunt for your ideal job, or even something close to your ideal job, you must have a picture of it, in your head. The clearer the picture, the easier it will be to hunt for it. The purpose of this exercise is to guide you as you draw that picture.

I have chosen a "Flower" as the model for that picture. While such expressions as "plugging in," "turning on," and other common phrases portray you (implicitly) as a machine, you are actually much more like a Flower than a machine. That is to say, you flourish in some job environments, but wither in others. Therefore, the purpose of putting together this Flower Diagram of yourself is to help you identify what kind of a work climate you will flourish in, and thus do your very best work. Your twin goals should be to be as happy as you can be at your job, while at the same time doing your most effective work.

There is a picture of the Flower on pages 2–3 that you can use as your worksheet.

As you can see, skills are at the center of the Flower, even as they are at the center of your mission, career, or job. They are listed in order of priority.

Surrounding them are six petals. Listed in the order in which you will work on them, they are:

1 Values

2 Special Knowledges

3 People-Environments

4 Working Conditions

5 Level of Responsibility and Salary

6 Geography

When you are done filling in these skills and petals, you will have the complete Flower Diagram of your Ideal Job. Okay? Then, get out your pen or pencil and let's get started.

The Flower

A PICTURE OF THE JOB OF YOUR DREAMS

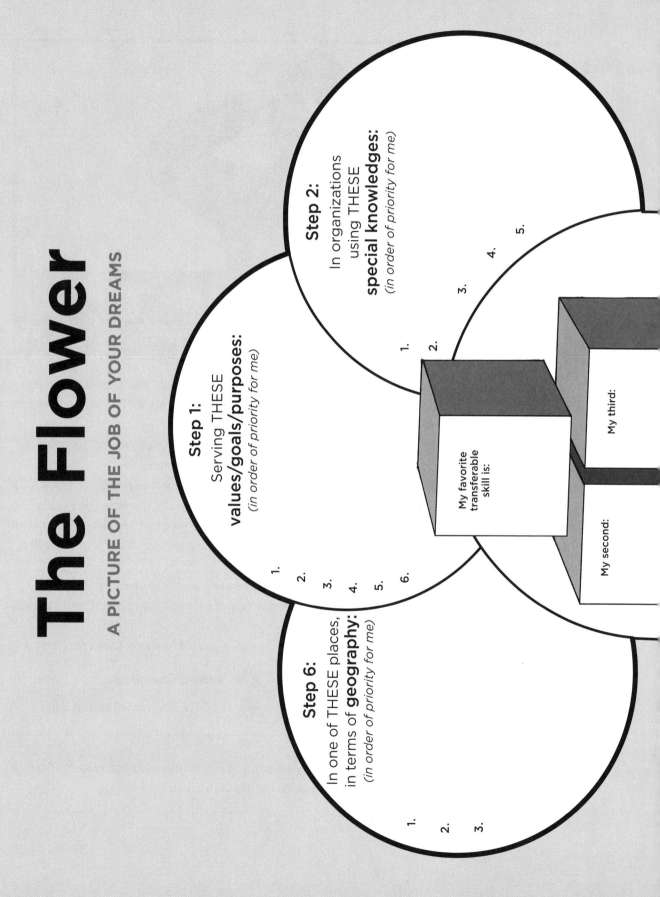

Step 1:
Serving THESE
values/goals/purposes:
(in order of priority for me)

1.
2.
3.
4.
5.
6.

Step 2:
In organizations
using THESE
special knowledges:
(in order of priority for me)

1.
2.
3.
4.
5.

Step 6:
In one of THESE places,
in terms of **geography:**
(in order of priority for me)

1.
2.
3.

My favorite transferable skill is:

My second:

My third:

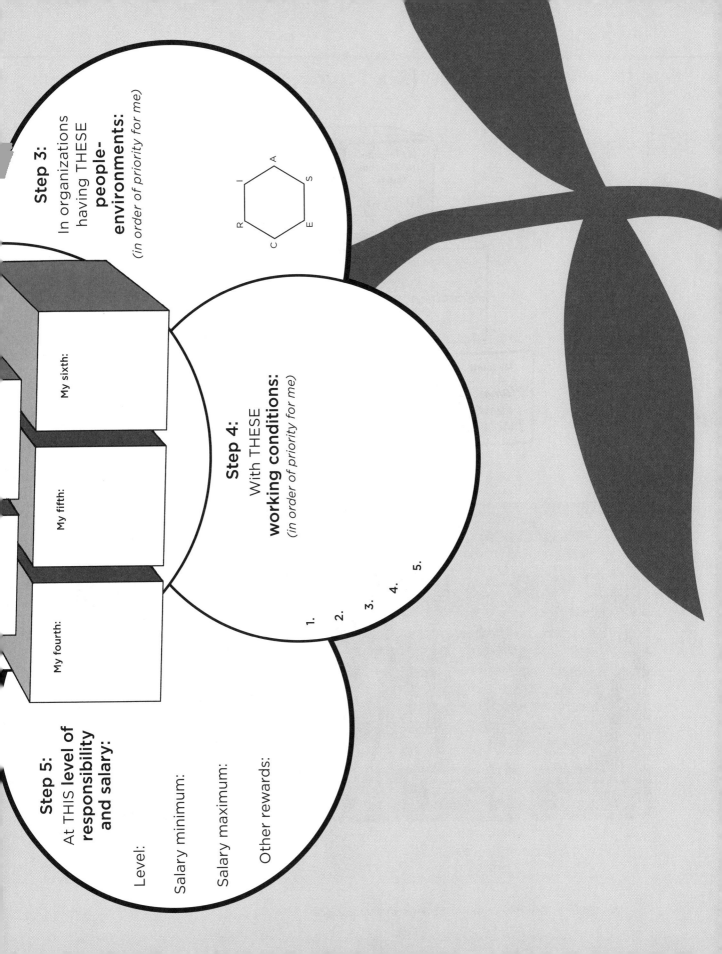

Step 3:
In organizations having THESE **people- environments:**
(in order of priority for me)

```
        A
    I       S

    R       E
        C
```

Step 4:
With THESE **working conditions:**
(in order of priority for me)

1.
2.
3.
4.
5.

My sixth:

My fifth:

My fourth:

Step 5:
At THIS **level of responsibility and salary:**

Level:

Salary minimum:

Salary maximum:

Other rewards:

Example (Six Favorite Skills)

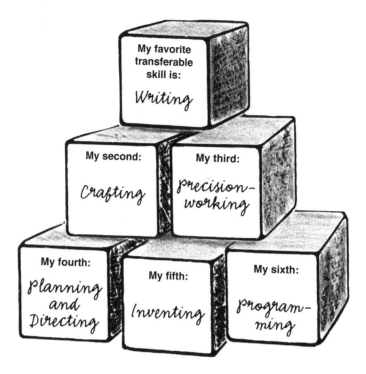

When it comes time to inventory what you have to offer to an employer, it's helpful to know that you basically have three different kinds of skills to offer them:

1. **Knowledge or Subject Skills**. These are usually nouns, like "computers," "applied mathematics," "dancing," "digital design," etc. Think of your head as a filing cabinet. You have a lot of knowledge stored in there, about various subjects. These make you an asset to particular companies. Because you can use these files, these are indeed skills.

2. **Functional or Transferable Skills**. These are usually verbs, like "analyzing," "mentoring," "cooking," etc. They are functions you are able to do. But because they are transferable to other fields, without going back to school for retraining, they are called transferable skills; e.g., if you're good at "gathering information," in one field, you're probably just as good at "gathering information" in another field. Completely transferable.

3. **Self-Management Skills, Often Called Traits**. These are usually adjectives or adverbs, like "systematic," or "persistent," or "thorough." They describe the manner in which you do some of your Transferable Skills.

We begin, here, with inventorying your Transferable Skills.

Your Favorite Transferable Skills

We begin with skills. You must, first of all, identify your favorite transferable skills that you most enjoy using, *in order of priority or importance to you*. Here are the five steps to accomplishing that.

1. Write Your First Story

To discover your favorite transferable skills, you will need to write seven stories about things you did just because they were fun, or because they gave you a sense of adventure, or gave you a sense of accomplishment. It does not matter whether anyone else ever knew about this accomplishment, or not. Each story can be about something you did at work, or in school, or at play—and can be from any time period of your life. It should not be more than two or three paragraphs in length.

SAMPLE (This won't do)
"The Halloween Experience. I won a prize on Halloween for dressing up as a horse."

SAMPLE (This will do)
"My Halloween Experience When I Was Seven Years Old. Details: When I was seven, I decided I wanted to go out on Halloween dressed as a horse. I wanted to be the front end of the horse, and I talked a friend of mine into being the back end of the horse. But, at the last moment he backed out, and I was faced with the prospect of not being able to go out on Halloween. At this point, I decided to figure out some way of getting dressed up as the whole horse, myself. I took a fruit basket, and tied some string to both sides of the basket's rim, so that I could tie the basket around my rear end. This filled me out enough so that the costume fit me, by myself. I then fixed some strong thread to the tail so that I could make it wag by moving my hands. When Halloween came I not only went out and had a ball, but I won a prize as well."

5

Below is a form to help you write the first of your Seven Stories. Use this form for notes, then write out the story on a separate piece of paper; don't try to confine it just to this form. After you have written your first story, I will show you how to analyze it for the transferable skills that you used therein.

MY FIRST LIFE STORY

Column 1	Column 2	Column 3	Column 4	Column 5
Your Goal (What you wanted to accomplish)	Some Kind of Obstacle (or limit, hurdle, or restraint) You Had to Overcome Before It Could Be Accomplished	What You Did Step-by-Step (It may help if you pretend you are telling this story to a whining 4-year-old child who keeps asking, after each of your sentences, "An' then whadja do? An' then whadja do?")	Description of the Result (What you accomplished)	Any Measure or Quantities to Prove Your Achievement

2. Analyze the Story for Transferable Skills

Once you have written Story #1 (and before you write the other six), you will want to analyze it for the transferable skills you *used*. (You can decide later if you loved those skills or not. For now, just do an inventory.)

To do this inventory, go to the lists of Skills Keys found on pages 8–10, which resemble a series of keyboard keys. Transferable skills divide into:

 Physical Skills: the transferable skills you enjoy, using primarily **your hands or body**—with things, or nature;

 Mental Skills: the transferable skills you enjoy, using primarily **your mind**—with data/information, ideas, or subjects;

3 Interpersonal Skills: the transferable skills you enjoy, involving primarily **personal relationships**—as you serve or help people or animals, and their needs or problems.[1]

Did I Use This Skill in Story

Therefore you will find three sets of Skills Keys, labeled accordingly.

As you look at each key in the three sets, the question you need to ask yourself is: "Did I use this transferable skill *in this Story* (**#1**)?"

That is the only question you ask yourself (at the moment). Then you go to the little box named #1 (under each Skill Key), and this is what you do:

If the answer is "Yes," fill in the little box, as shown (left). Ignore the other little boxes for the time being; they belong to your other stories (all the little boxes named #2 belong to Story #2, all the little boxes named #3 belong to Story #3, etc.).

Did I Use This Skill in Story

If the answer is "No," leave the box labeled #1 blank, as shown (right).

If you run into any problems, see the troubleshooting section starting on page 23 for help.

3. Write Six Other Stories, and Analyze Them for Transferable Skills

Voilà! You are done with Story #1. However, "one swallow doth not a summer make," so the fact that you used certain skills in this first Story doesn't tell you much. You are looking for patterns—transferable skills that keep reappearing in story after story. They keep reappearing because they are your favorites (assuming you chose stories where you were really enjoying yourself).

So, now, write Story #2, from any period in your life, analyze it using the keys, etc., etc. And keep this process up, until you have written, and analyzed, seven stories (using the blank forms that follow, starting on page 11).

---

1. For the curious, "animals" are placed in this category with "people," because the skills required to deal with animals are more like those used with people, than like those used with "things."

My Physical Skills

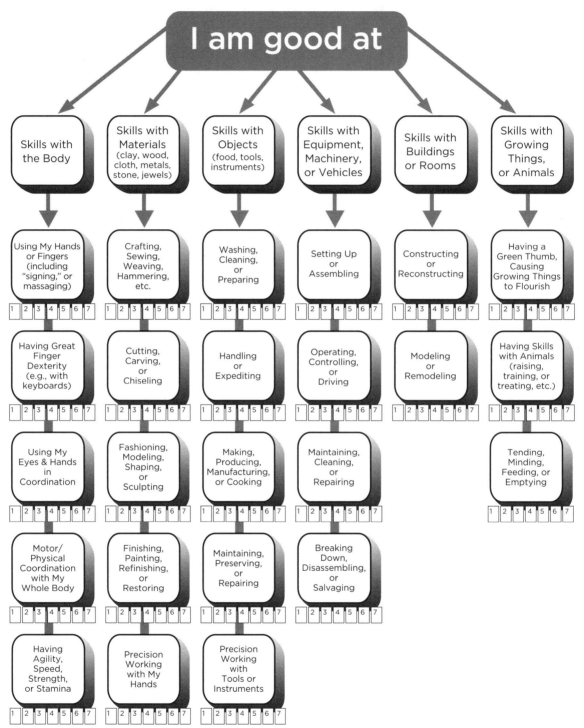

I am good at

Skills with the Body
- Using My Hands or Fingers (including "signing," or massaging) — 1 2 3 4 5 6 7
- Having Great Finger Dexterity (e.g., with keyboards) — 1 2 3 4 5 6 7
- Using My Eyes & Hands in Coordination — 1 2 3 4 5 6 7
- Motor/Physical Coordination with My Whole Body — 1 2 3 4 5 6 7
- Having Agility, Speed, Strength, or Stamina — 1 2 3 4 5 6 7

Skills with Materials (clay, wood, cloth, metals, stone, jewels)
- Crafting, Sewing, Weaving, Hammering, etc. — 1 2 3 4 5 6 7
- Cutting, Carving, or Chiseling — 1 2 3 4 5 6 7
- Fashioning, Modeling, Shaping, or Sculpting — 1 2 3 4 5 6 7
- Finishing, Painting, Refinishing, or Restoring — 1 2 3 4 5 6 7
- Precision Working with My Hands — 1 2 3 4 5 6 7

Skills with Objects (food, tools, instruments)
- Washing, Cleaning, or Preparing — 1 2 3 4 5 6 7
- Handling or Expediting — 1 2 3 4 5 6 7
- Making, Producing, Manufacturing, or Cooking — 1 2 3 4 5 6 7
- Maintaining, Preserving, or Repairing — 1 2 3 4 5 6 7
- Precision Working with Tools or Instruments — 1 2 3 4 5 6 7

Skills with Equipment, Machinery, or Vehicles
- Setting Up or Assembling — 1 2 3 4 5 6 7
- Operating, Controlling, or Driving — 1 2 3 4 5 6 7
- Maintaining, Cleaning, or Repairing — 1 2 3 4 5 6 7
- Breaking Down, Disassembling, or Salvaging — 1 2 3 4 5 6 7

Skills with Buildings or Rooms
- Constructing or Reconstructing — 1 2 3 4 5 6 7
- Modeling or Remodeling — 1 2 3 4 5 6 7

Skills with Growing Things, or Animals
- Having a Green Thumb, Causing Growing Things to Flourish — 1 2 3 4 5 6 7
- Having Skills with Animals (raising, training, or treating, etc.) — 1 2 3 4 5 6 7
- Tending, Minding, Feeding, or Emptying — 1 2 3 4 5 6 7

My Mental Skills

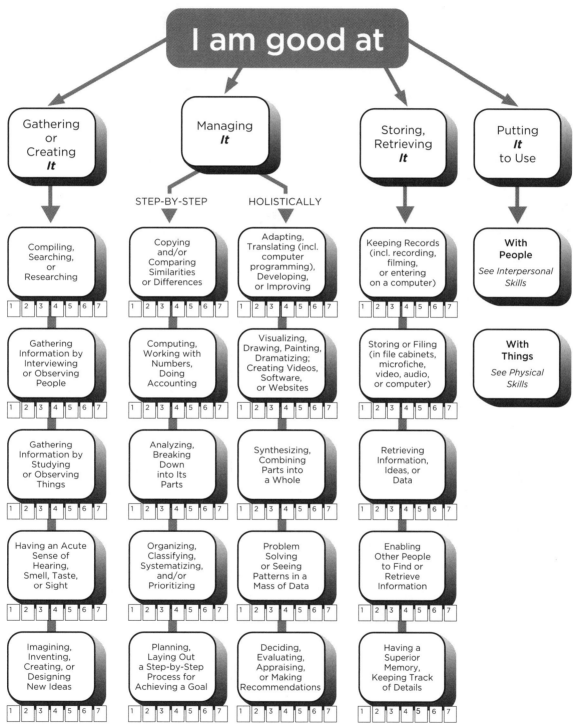

I am good at

Gathering or Creating It

Managing It

STEP-BY-STEP   HOLISTICALLY

Storing, Retrieving It

Putting It to Use

Gathering or Creating It	Managing It (Step-by-Step)	Managing It (Holistically)	Storing, Retrieving It	Putting It to Use
Compiling, Searching, or Researching	Copying and/or Comparing Similarities or Differences	Adapting, Translating (incl. computer programming), Developing, or Improving	Keeping Records (incl. recording, filming, or entering on a computer)	**With People** *See Interpersonal Skills*
Gathering Information by Interviewing or Observing People	Computing, Working with Numbers, Doing Accounting	Visualizing, Drawing, Painting, Dramatizing; Creating Videos, Software, or Websites	Storing or Filing (in file cabinets, microfiche, video, audio, or computer)	**With Things** *See Physical Skills*
Gathering Information by Studying or Observing Things	Analyzing, Breaking Down into Its Parts	Synthesizing, Combining Parts into a Whole	Retrieving Information, Ideas, or Data	
Having an Acute Sense of Hearing, Smell, Taste, or Sight	Organizing, Classifying, Systematizing, and/or Prioritizing	Problem Solving or Seeing Patterns in a Mass of Data	Enabling Other People to Find or Retrieve Information	
Imagining, Inventing, Creating, or Designing New Ideas	Planning, Laying Out a Step-by-Step Process for Achieving a Goal	Deciding, Evaluating, Appraising, or Making Recommendations	Having a Superior Memory, Keeping Track of Details	

Each box has a rating scale: 1 2 3 4 5 6 7

My Interpersonal Skills

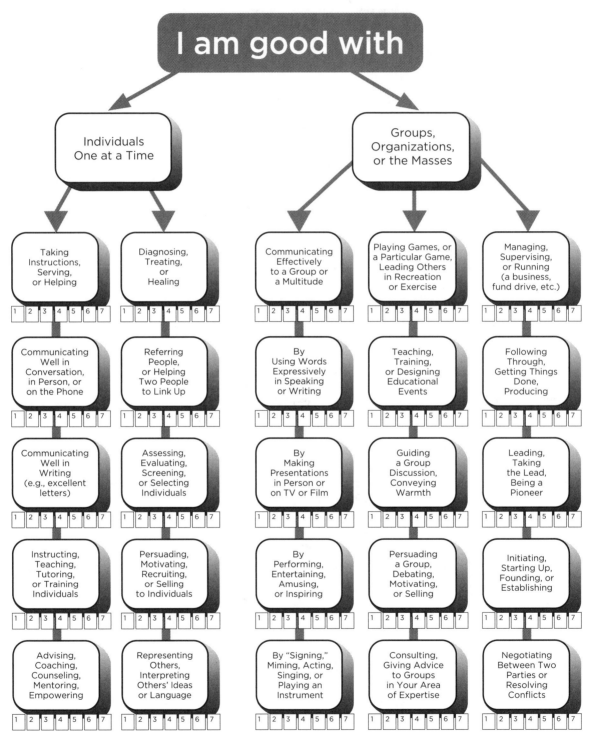

I am good with

Individuals One at a Time

Taking Instructions, Serving, or Helping
1 2 3 4 5 6 7

Communicating Well in Conversation, in Person, or on the Phone
1 2 3 4 5 6 7

Communicating Well in Writing (e.g., excellent letters)
1 2 3 4 5 6 7

Instructing, Teaching, Tutoring, or Training Individuals
1 2 3 4 5 6 7

Advising, Coaching, Counseling, Mentoring, Empowering
1 2 3 4 5 6 7

Diagnosing, Treating, or Healing
1 2 3 4 5 6 7

Referring People, or Helping Two People to Link Up
1 2 3 4 5 6 7

Assessing, Evaluating, Screening, or Selecting Individuals
1 2 3 4 5 6 7

Persuading, Motivating, Recruiting, or Selling to Individuals
1 2 3 4 5 6 7

Representing Others, Interpreting Others' Ideas or Language
1 2 3 4 5 6 7

Groups, Organizations, or the Masses

Communicating Effectively to a Group or a Multitude
1 2 3 4 5 6 7

By Using Words Expressively in Speaking or Writing
1 2 3 4 5 6 7

By Making Presentations in Person or on TV or Film
1 2 3 4 5 6 7

By Performing, Entertaining, Amusing, or Inspiring
1 2 3 4 5 6 7

By "Signing," Miming, Acting, Singing, or Playing an Instrument
1 2 3 4 5 6 7

Playing Games, or a Particular Game, Leading Others in Recreation or Exercise
1 2 3 4 5 6 7

Teaching, Training, or Designing Educational Events
1 2 3 4 5 6 7

Guiding a Group Discussion, Conveying Warmth
1 2 3 4 5 6 7

Persuading a Group, Debating, Motivating, or Selling
1 2 3 4 5 6 7

Consulting, Giving Advice to Groups in Your Area of Expertise
1 2 3 4 5 6 7

Managing, Supervising, or Running (a business, fund drive, etc.)
1 2 3 4 5 6 7

Following Through, Getting Things Done, Producing
1 2 3 4 5 6 7

Leading, Taking the Lead, Being a Pioneer
1 2 3 4 5 6 7

Initiating, Starting Up, Founding, or Establishing
1 2 3 4 5 6 7

Negotiating Between Two Parties or Resolving Conflicts
1 2 3 4 5 6 7

MY SECOND LIFE STORY

Column 1	Column 2	Column 3	Column 4	Column 5
Your Goal (What you wanted to accomplish)	Some Kind of Obstacle (or limit, hurdle, or restraint) You Had to Overcome Before It Could Be Accomplished	What You Did Step-by-Step (It may help if you pretend you are telling this story to a whining 4-year-old child who keeps asking, after each of your sentences, "An' then whadja do? An' then whadja do?")	Description of the Result (What you accomplished)	Any Measure or Quantities to Prove Your Achievement

MY THIRD LIFE STORY

Column 1	Column 2	Column 3	Column 4	Column 5
Your Goal (What you wanted to accomplish)	Some Kind of Obstacle (or limit, hurdle, or restraint) You Had to Overcome Before It Could Be Accomplished	What You Did Step-by-Step (It may help if you pretend you are telling this story to a whining 4-year-old child who keeps asking, after each of your sentences, "An' then whadja do? An' then whadja do?")	Description of the Result (What you accomplished)	Any Measure or Quantities to Prove Your Achievement

MY FOURTH LIFE STORY

Column 1	Column 2	Column 3	Column 4	Column 5
Your Goal (What you wanted to accomplish)	Some Kind of Obstacle (or limit, hurdle, or restraint) You Had to Overcome Before It Could Be Accomplished	What You Did Step-by-Step (It may help if you pretend you are telling this story to a whining 4-year-old child who keeps asking, after each of your sentences, "An' then whadja do? An' then whadja do?")	Description of the Result (What you accomplished)	Any Measure or Quantities to Prove Your Achievement

MY FIFTH LIFE STORY

Column 1	Column 2	Column 3	Column 4	Column 5
Your Goal (What you wanted to accomplish)	Some Kind of Obstacle (or limit, hurdle, or restraint) You Had to Overcome Before It Could Be Accomplished	What You Did Step-by-Step (It may help if you pretend you are telling this story to a whining 4-year-old child who keeps asking, after each of your sentences, "An' then whadja do? An' then whadja do?")	Description of the Result (What you accomplished)	Any Measure or Quantities to Prove Your Achievement

MY SIXTH LIFE STORY

Column 1	Column 2	Column 3	Column 4	Column 5
Your Goal (What you wanted to accomplish)	Some Kind of Obstacle (or limit, hurdle, or restraint) You Had to Overcome Before It Could Be Accomplished	What You Did Step-by-Step (It may help if you pretend you are telling this story to a whining 4-year-old child who keeps asking, after each of your sentences, "An' then whadja do? An' then whadja do?")	Description of the Result (What you accomplished)	Any Measure or Quantities to Prove Your Achievement

MY SEVENTH LIFE STORY

Column 1	Column 2	Column 3	Column 4	Column 5
Your Goal (What you wanted to accomplish)	Some Kind of Obstacle (or limit, hurdle, or restraint) You Had to Overcome Before It Could Be Accomplished	What You Did Step-by-Step (It may help if you pretend you are telling this story to a whining 4-year-old child who keeps asking, after each of your sentences, "An' then whadja do? An' then whadja do?")	Description of the Result (What you accomplished)	Any Measure or Quantities to Prove Your Achievement

4. Decide Which Skills Are Your Favorites, and Prioritize Them

When you're done writing and analyzing all Seven Stories, you should now go back and look over the three pages of "Skills Keys" to see which skills got used the most often. Make a list.

Cross out any that you don't enjoy using. See if you can get your favorite skills down to about ten, just by guess and by gosh; then arrange those ten in precise order, from your favorite to your least favorite, using the 10-item Prioritizing Grid on page 19. If you just can't get your favorites down to ten, then use the 24-item Grid (or any part of it) on page 17, here.

```
1  1  1  1  1  1  1  1  1  1  1  1  1  1  1  1  1  1  1  1  1  1  1
  2  3  4  5  6  7  8  9  10 11 12 13 14 15 16 17 18 19 20 21 22 23 24

2  2  2  2  2  2  2  2  2  2  2  2  2  2  2  2  2  2  2  2  2  2
  3  4  5  6  7  8  9  10 11 12 13 14 15 16 17 18 19 20 21 22 23 24

3  3  3  3  3  3  3  3  3  3  3  3  3  3  3  3  3  3  3  3  3
  4  5  6  7  8  9  10 11 12 13 14 15 16 17 18 19 20 21 22 23 24

4  4  4  4  4  4  4  4  4  4  4  4  4  4  4  4  4  4  4  4
  5  6  7  8  9  10 11 12 13 14 15 16 17 18 19 20 21 22 23 24

5  5  5  5  5  5  5  5  5  5  5  5  5  5  5  5  5  5  5
  6  7  8  9  10 11 12 13 14 15 16 17 18 19 20 21 22 23 24

6  6  6  6  6  6  6  6  6  6  6  6  6  6  6  6  6  6
  7  8  9  10 11 12 13 14 15 16 17 18 19 20 21 22 23 24

7  7  7  7  7  7  7  7  7  7  7  7  7  7  7  7  7
  8  9  10 11 12 13 14 15 16 17 18 19 20 21 22 23 24

8  8  8  8  8  8  8  8  8  8  8  8  8  8  8  8
  9  10 11 12 13 14 15 16 17 18 19 20 21 22 23 24

9  9  9  9  9  9  9  9  9  9  9  9  9  9  9
  10 11 12 13 14 15 16 17 18 19 20 21 22 23 24

10 10 10 10 10 10 10 10 10 10 10 10 10 10
  11 12 13 14 15 16 17 18 19 20 21 22 23 24

11 11 11 11 11 11 11 11 11 11 11 11 11
  12 13 14 15 16 17 18 19 20 21 22 23 24

12 12 12 12 12 12 12 12 12 12 12 12
  13 14 15 16 17 18 19 20 21 22 23 24

13 13 13 13 13 13 13 13 13 13 13
  14 15 16 17 18 19 20 21 22 23 24

14 14 14 14 14 14 14 14 14 14
  15 16 17 18 19 20 21 22 23 24

15 15 15 15 15 15 15 15 15
  16 17 18 19 20 21 22 23 24

16 16 16 16 16 16 16 16
  17 18 19 20 21 22 23 24

17 17 17 17 17 17 17
  18 19 20 21 22 23 24

18 18 18 18 18 18
  19 20 21 22 23 24

19 19 19 19 19
  20 21 22 23 24

20 20 20 20
  21 22 23 24

21 21 21
  22 23 24

22 22
  23 24

23
  24
```

Total times each number got circled.

1	2	3	4	5	6
7	8	9	10	11	12
13	14	15	16	17	18
19	20	21	22	23	24

OPTIONAL PRIORITIZING GRID FOR 24 ITEMS

The Prioritizing Grid
HOW TO PRIORITIZE YOUR LISTS OF ANYTHING

Here is a method for taking, say, ten items, and figuring out which one is most important to you, which is next most important, etc.

- Insert the items to be prioritized, in any order, in Section A of the Prioritizing Grid on page 19, here. Then compare just two items at a time, circling the one you prefer—between the two—in Section B. Which one is more important to you? State the question any way you want to: In the case of your functional/transferable skills, you might ask, with each pair, "If I were being offered two jobs, one where I could use skill #1, but not skill #2, the other job where I could use skill #2, but not skill #1, which job would I take?" Circle it. Then go on to the next pair, etc.

- When you are all done, count up the number of times each number got circled, all told. Enter these totals on the TIMES line in Section C. Then notice the number of times each item was circled ("Times" = "Times Circled"). This determines the item's ranking. Most circled = #1, next most circled = #2, etc. Enter this ranking on the RANK line in Section C. If two items are circled the same number of times, look back in Section B to see—when those two were compared there—which one you preferred. Give that one an extra half point. List the items, now in their proper rank, in Section D. When you've got your ten favorite transferable skills, in order, copy the top six onto the Flower Diagram on pages 2–3.

Although I include a number of Prioritizing Grids in this workbook for you to fill out, you might want to make some extra photocopies before you get started–especially of the 24-item Grid, which is included less often than the standard 10-item Grid. You can also try an interactive electronic version of the Prioritizing Grid at www.GroundOfYourOwnChoosing.com, the website of a former student of mine, Beverly Ryle, now a noted career counselor and author.

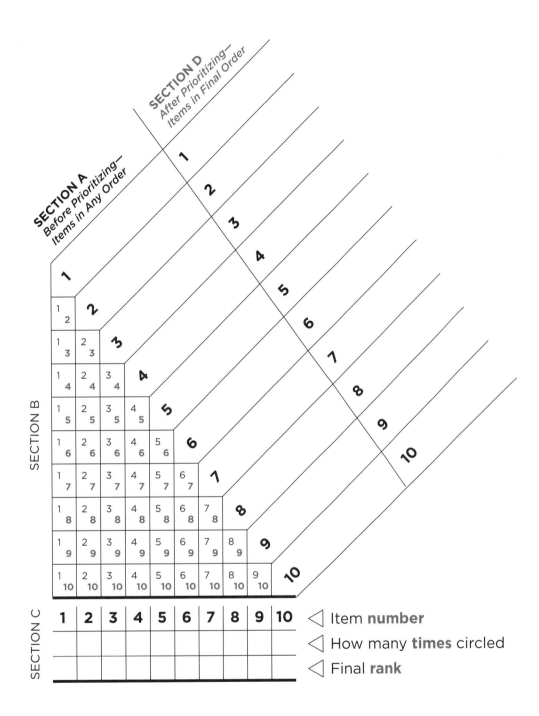

SECTION B

	1									

SECTION A — Before Prioritizing — Items in Any Order

1

1/2   2

1/3   2/3   3

1/4   2/4   3/4   4

1/5   2/5   3/5   4/5   5

1/6   2/6   3/6   4/6   5/6   6

1/7   2/7   3/7   4/7   5/7   6/7   7

1/8   2/8   3/8   4/8   5/8   6/8   7/8   8

1/9   2/9   3/9   4/9   5/9   6/9   7/9   8/9   9

1/10   2/10   3/10   4/10   5/10   6/10   7/10   8/10   9/10   10

SECTION D — After Prioritizing — Items in Final Order
1 2 3 4 5 6 7 8 9 10

SECTION C

1	2	3	4	5	6	7	8	9	10

◁ Item **number**

◁ How many **times** circled

◁ Final **rank**

PRIORITIZING GRID FOR 10 ITEMS

5. "Flesh Out" Your Favorite Transferable Skills with Your Traits

Traits are often mistaken for skills. When asked their skills, people will often reply, "Persistence, thoroughness, intuitiveness"—that sort of thing. Actually, traits are *modifiers* of your functional, transferable skills; they describe how you do those skills, hence they are mostly adjectives or adverbs. In general, traits describe:

- How you deal with time, and promptness.
- How you deal with people and emotions.
- How you deal with authority, and being told what to do at your job.
- How you deal with supervision, and being told how to do your job.
- How you deal with impulse vs. self-discipline, within yourself.
- How you deal with initiative vs. response, within yourself.
- How you deal with crises or problems.

In other words, traits describe **how** you perform your transferable skills. Once you've checked off your favorite traits in the list below, prioritize them (using the Prioritizing Grid on page 22 if necessary), and then write in your favorites where it seems most appropriate, on the building blocks of transferable skills on your Flower Diagram.

A CHECKLIST OF MY STRONGEST TRAITS
I am very . . .

❑ Accurate	❑ Competent
❑ Achievement-oriented	❑ Consistent
❑ Adaptable	❑ Contagious in my enthusiasm
❑ Adept	❑ Cooperative
❑ Adventurous	❑ Courageous
❑ Alert	❑ Creative
❑ Appreciative	❑ Decisive
❑ Assertive	❑ Deliberate
❑ Astute	❑ Dependable
❑ Authoritative	❑ Diligent
❑ Calm	❑ Diplomatic
❑ Cautious	❑ Discreet
❑ Charismatic	❑ Driving

- ❑ Dynamic
- ❑ Economical
- ❑ Effective
- ❑ Energetic
- ❑ Enthusiastic
- ❑ Exceptional
- ❑ Exhaustive
- ❑ Experienced
- ❑ Expert
- ❑ Firm
- ❑ Flexible
- ❑ Fun-loving
- ❑ Humanly oriented
- ❑ Impulsive
- ❑ Independent
- ❑ Innovative
- ❑ Knowledgeable
- ❑ Loyal
- ❑ Methodical
- ❑ Objective
- ❑ Open-minded
- ❑ Outgoing
- ❑ Outstanding
- ❑ Patient
- ❑ Penetrating
- ❑ Perceptive
- ❑ Persevering
- ❑ Persistent
- ❑ Pioneering
- ❑ Practical
- ❑ Professional
- ❑ Protective

- ❑ Punctual
- ❑ Quick/work quickly
- ❑ Rational
- ❑ Realistic
- ❑ Reliable
- ❑ Resourceful
- ❑ Responsible
- ❑ Responsive
- ❑ Safeguarding
- ❑ Self-motivated
- ❑ Self-reliant
- ❑ Sensitive
- ❑ Sophisticated, very sophisticated
- ❑ Strong
- ❑ Supportive
- ❑ Tactful
- ❑ Thorough
- ❑ Unique
- ❑ Unusual
- ❑ Versatile
- ❑ Vigorous

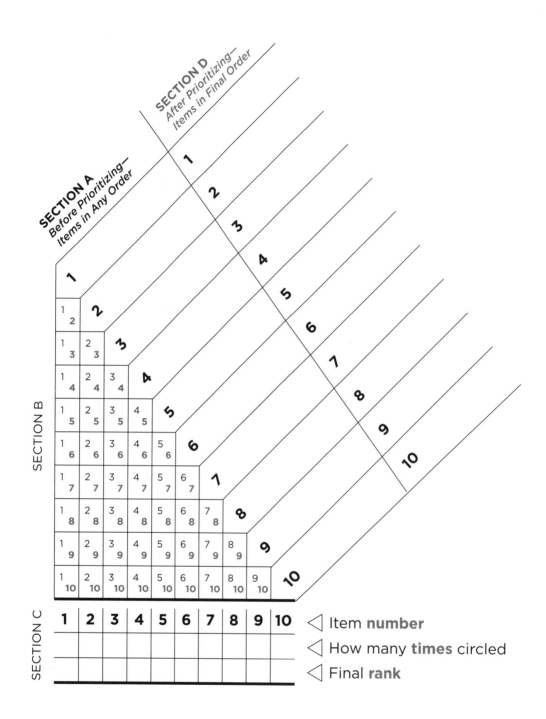

PRIORITIZING GRID FOR 10 ITEMS

Some Problems You May Run Into, While Doing Your Skill-Identification

In trying to identify your skills on the previous pages, it will not be surprising if you run into some problems. Let us look at the five most common ones that have arisen for job-hunters in the past:

1 *"When I write my skill stories, I don't know exactly what is an achievement."*

When you're looking for a story/achievement to illustrate one of your skills, you're *not* looking for something that only you have done, in the history of the world. What you're looking for is a lot simpler than that. You're looking for *any* time in your life when you did something that was, at that time of your life, a source of pride and accomplishment *for you*. It might have been learning to ride a bike. It might be achieving your first quota, at work. It might be a particularly significant project that you designed, in midlife. It doesn't matter whether or not it pleased anybody else; it only matters that it pleased you.

I like Bernard Haldane's definition of an achievement. He said it is: something you yourself feel you have done well, that you also enjoyed doing and felt proud of. In other words, you are looking for an accomplishment that gave you two pleasures: enjoyment while doing it, and satisfaction from the outcome. That doesn't mean you may not have sweated as you did it, or hated *some parts* of the process, but it does mean that basically you enjoyed *most of* the process. The pleasure was not simply in the outcome, but along the way as well.

2 *"I don't see why I should look for skills I enjoy; it seems to me that employers will only want to know what skills I do well. They will not care whether I enjoy using the skill or not."*

Well, sure, it is important for you to find the skills you do well, above all else. But, generally speaking, that is hard for you to evaluate about yourself. *Do I do this well, or not? Compared to whom?* Even aptitude tests can't resolve this dilemma for you. So it's better to take the following circular equation, which experience has shown to be true:

If it is a skill you do well, you will generally enjoy it.

If it is a skill you enjoy, it is generally because you do it well.

With these equations in hand, you will see that—since they are equal anyway—it is much more useful to ask yourself, "Do I enjoy doing it?" instead of hunting for the elusive "Do I do it well?" I repeat: listing the skills you most *enjoy* is—in most cases—just another way of listing the skills you do *best*.

The reason why this idea—of making *enjoyment* the key—causes such feelings of uncomfortableness in so many of us is that we have an old historical tradition in this country that insinuates you shouldn't really enjoy yourself in life. To suffer is virtuous.

Sample: Two girls do babysitting. One hates it. One enjoys it thoroughly. Which is more virtuous in God's sight? According to that old tradition, the one who hates it is more virtuous. Some of us feel this instinctively, even if more logical thought says, Whoa!

We have this subconscious fear that if we are caught enjoying life, punishment looms. Thus, the story of two Scotsmen who met on the street one day: "Isn't this a beautiful day?" said one. "Aye," said the other, "but we'll pay for it."

We feel it is okay to talk about our failures, but not about our successes. To talk about our successes appears to be boasting, and that is manifestly a sin. Or so we think. We shouldn't be enjoying so much about ourselves.

But look at the birds of the air, or watch your pets at play. You will notice one distinctive fact about that part of God's creation: when a bird or a pet does what it is meant to do, by God and nature, it manifests true joy. *(When I see these things, I view them through the lens of my personal faith in God—I was ordained as a minister, after all—but if you are of a different spiritual persuasion, which of course I welcome and celebrate, you'll still understand what I'm getting at, here.)*

Joy is so clearly a part of God's plan for us. God wants us to eat; therefore, He made eating enjoyable. God wants us to sleep; therefore, He made sleeping enjoyable. God wants us to procreate, love, and make love; therefore, He made sex enjoyable, and love even more so.

Likewise, God gives to each of us unique combinations of skills and talents that He wants us to contribute to His general plan—to the symphony of the world, and the music of the spheres. Therefore, when we use the talents He most wants each of us to use, He attends it with a feeling of great joy. Everywhere in God's plan for His creation, joy rewards right action.

Bad employers will not care whether you enjoy a particular task, or not. But good employers will care greatly. They know that unless a would-be employee has **enthusiasm** for his or her work, the quality of that work will always suffer.

3 *"I have no difficulty finding stories to write up, from my life, that I consider to be enjoyable achievements; but once these are written, I have great difficulty in seeing what the skills are—even if I stare at the Skill Keys for hours. I need somebody else's insight."*

You may want to consider getting two friends or two other members of your family to sit down with you, and do skill identification through the practice of "Trioing," which I invented some twenty years ago to help with this very problem. This practice is fully described in my book *Where Do I Go from Here with My Life?* But to save you the trouble of hunting down that book, here is—in general—how it goes:

a. Each of the three of you quietly writes up some story of an accomplishment in your life that was enjoyable.

b. Each of the three of you quietly analyzes just your own story to see which skills you see there; you jot these down.

c. One of you then volunteers to go first. You read your story aloud. The other two jot down on a piece of paper whichever skills they hear you using. They ask you to pause if they're having trouble keeping up. You finish your story. You read aloud the skills *you* picked out in that story.

d. Then the second person tells you what's on their list: which skills *they* heard you use in your story. You copy them down, below your own list, even if you don't agree with every one of them.

e. Then the third person tells you what's on their list: which skills *they* heard you use in your story. You copy them down, below your own list, even if you don't agree with every one of them.

f. When they're both done, you ask them any questions for further elaboration that you may have. *"What did you mean by this skill? Where did you think you heard me using it?"*

g. Now it is the next person's turn, and you repeat steps "c" through "f" with them. Then it is the third person's turn, and you repeat steps "c" through "f" with them.

h. Now it is time to move on to a second story for each of you, so you begin with steps "a" through "g" all over again, except that each of you writes a new story. And so on, through seven stories.

4 *"I don't like the skill words you offer. Can't I use my own words, the ones I'm familiar with from my past profession?"*

It's okay to invent your own words for your skills, but it is not useful to state your transferable skills in the jargon of your old profession, such as (in the case of ex-clergy) *"I am good at preaching."* If you are going to choose a new career out there in what people call the secular world, you must not use language that locks you into the past—or suggests that you were good in one profession but in that profession only. Therefore, it is important to take jargon words such as *preaching* and ask yourself, What is its larger form? *"Teaching?"* Perhaps. *"Motivating people?"* Perhaps. *"Inspiring people to the depths of their being?"* Perhaps. Only you can say what is true, for you. But in one way or another, be sure to get your skills out of any jargon that locks you into your past career.

5 *"Once I've listed my favorite transferable skills, I see immediately a job-title that they point to. Is that okay?"*

Nope. Once you've finished your skill-identification, steer clear of prematurely putting a job-title on the skills you see. Skills can point to *many* different jobs, which have a multitude of titles. Therefore, don't lock yourself in, prematurely. *"I'm looking for a job where I can* use *the following skills,"* is fine. But, *"I'm looking for a job where I can* be *a (job-title)"* is a no-no, at this point in your job-hunt. Always define **WHAT** you want to do with your life and **WHAT** you have to offer to the world, in terms of your favorite talents/gifts/skills—not in terms of a job-title. That way, you can stay mobile in the midst of this constantly changing economy, where you never know what's going to happen next.

Petal #1: **Your Favorite Values**

Values are a matter of what guides you through every day, every task, every encounter with another human being. Yet, we are often unaware of what our values are.

One way to bring values to your consciousness is to imagine that shortly before the end of your life you are invited to dinner—and to your great surprise people have secretly come in from all over the country and all over the world, to attend a surprise testimonial dinner for You.

At the dinner, to your great embarrassment, there is one testimonial after another about the good things you did, or the good person that you were, in your lifetime. No mention of any parts of your life that you don't want to have remembered. Just the good stuff.

So, this brings us to some questions. If you get the life you really want between now and then, what would you hope you would hear at that dinner, as the guests looked back on your life?

If you do achieve what you want with your life, what about you would you like to have remembered, after you are gone from this earth? Below is a checklist to help you.[2]

It would be a good life, if at its end, people remembered me as one who (check as many items as are important to you):

- ❏ Served or helped those who were in need.
- ❏ Impressed people with my going the extra mile, in meeting their needs.
- ❏ Was always a great listener.
- ❏ Was always good at carrying out orders, or bringing projects to a successful conclusion.

- ❏ Mastered some technique, or field.
- ❏ Did something that everyone said couldn't be done.
- ❏ Did something that no one had ever done before.
- ❏ Excelled and was the best at whatever it is I did.

2. I am indebted to Arthur Miller, of People Management, Inc., for many of these ideas.

- ❑ Pioneered or explored some new technology.
- ❑ Fixed something that was broken.
- ❑ Made something work, when everyone else had failed or given up.
- ❑ Improved something, made it better, or perfected it.
- ❑ Combatted some bad idea/philosophy/force/influence/pervasive trend—and I persevered and/or prevailed.
- ❑ Influenced people and gained a tremendous response from them.
- ❑ Had an impact, and caused change.
- ❑ Did work that brought more information/truth into the world.
- ❑ Did work that brought more beauty into the world, through gardens, or painting, or decorating, or designing, or whatever.
- ❑ Did work that brought more justice, truth, and ethical behavior into the world.
- ❑ Brought people closer to God or spirituality.
- ❑ Grew in wisdom and compassion, my great goal all my life.
- ❑ Had a vision of what something could be, and helped that vision come true.

- ❑ Developed or built something, where there was nothing.
- ❑ Began a new business, or did some project from start to finish.
- ❑ Exploited, shaped, and influenced some situation, or market, before others saw the potential.
- ❑ Put together a great team, which made a huge difference in its field, industry, or community.
- ❑ Was a good decision maker.
- ❑ Was acknowledged by everyone as a leader, and was in charge of whatever it was that I was doing.
- ❑ Had status in my field, industry, or community.
- ❑ Was in the spotlight, gained recognition, and was well known.
- ❑ Made it into a higher echelon than I was in, in terms of reputation, and/or prestige, and/or membership, and/or salary.
- ❑ Was able to acquire possessions, things, or money.
- ❑ Other goals that occur to me:

———————————————————

———————————————————

———————————————————

When you're done checking off all the values that are important to you, go back, and pick out the ten that you care the most about, and then prioritize them in exact order of importance to you. As always, if you just can't prioritize them by guess and by gosh, then use the Prioritizing Grid on page 28.

The question to ask yourself, there, as you confront each "pair" on the Grid is: "If I could only have this true about me, at the end of my life, but not the other, which would I prefer?" *Try not to pay attention to what others might or might not think of you, if they knew this was your heart's desire. This is just between you and your Creator.*

Put your top six values on the Values petal, in the Flower Diagram on pages 2–3.

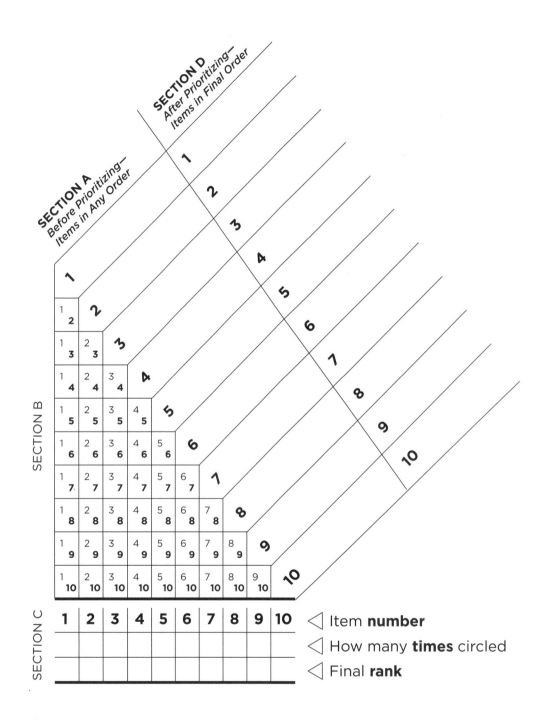

SECTION D
*After Prioritizing—
Items in Final Order*

SECTION A
*Before Prioritizing—
Items in Any Order*

SECTION B

SECTION C	1	2	3	4	5	6	7	8	9	10

◁ Item **number**

◁ How many **times** circled

◁ Final **rank**

PRIORITIZING GRID FOR 10 ITEMS

Petal #2: **Your Favorite Special Knowledges, or "Fields of Fascination"**

Now we move from the question of WHAT (What transferable skills of yours do you most enjoy using?) to the question of WHERE (Where would you most like to use those skills?). In other words, we are talking particularly about Fields, here, and the Fields that fascinate you the most, as a place for you to work.

Now, there are three basic kinds of Fields that may fascinate you, in which you have some Special Knowledge or even mastery:

1. Subjects (these are fields that depend heavily on your information skills)

2. People Problems (these are fields that depend heavily on your interpersonal skills)

3. Things, Tools, or Products (these are fields that depend heavily on your physical skills)

Let us do some exercises, dealing with each of them in turn.

Before you begin looking at Fields, you must fight against the natural tendency to think that a Field will automatically determine what job you will do. It does not.

Think of a Field of Special Knowledge as, literally, a field—a meadow, a large meadow. Lots of people are standing in that meadow, or Field, no matter what Field it is. And they have many different skills, do many different things, have many different job-titles.

Let us take the Field called "Movies" as our example. Suppose you love Movies, and want to choose this Field for your next job or career. Your first instinct will be to think that this automatically means you have to be either an actor or actress, or a screenwriter, or a director, or a movie critic. Not so. There are many other people standing out in that Field, helping to produce Movies. Just look at the closing credits at the end of any movie, and you will see: researchers (especially for movies set in another time), travel experts (to scout locations), interior designers (to design sets), carpenters (to build them), painters (for backdrops, etc.), artists, computer graphics designers (for special effects), costume designers, makeup artists, hairstylists, photographers (camera operators), lighting technicians, sound mixers and sound editors, composers (for soundtracks), conductors, musicians, singers, stunt people, animal trainers, caterers, drivers, first aid people, personal assistants, secretaries, publicists, accountants, etc., etc. My, there are a lot of people standing in that Field—some of whom are outstanding in their Field!

And so it is with any Field. No matter what your skills are, they can be used in any meadow or Field that you may choose as your favorite.

1. Fields That Use Your Mental Skills

For some people, incidentally, Subjects yield the least helpful information about future Fields. Reason? Subjects often don't point to jobs. Example? Liberal Arts. But, might as well inventory everything we've learned so far, just in case (using the exercise called **The Subjects Chart** on page 32). Then you can go on to the exercise called **The People List** on page 35, and then the exercise called **The Things Phone Book** on page 39.

Everyone has mental skills.

Your mental skills are such things as: *the ability to gather information, to analyze information, to organize information, to present information,* and the like. The question here is: **what kinds of information, subjects, bodies of knowledge, ideas, or languages do you like to use your mental skills with?**

In order for you to answer this question, it is helpful to fill out the following chart; *you may first copy it onto a larger piece of paper, if you wish, in order to have more room to write.*

Please note that this chart is asking you what subjects you know anything about, whether you like the subject or not. (*Later,* you will ask yourself which of these you like or even *love.*) For now, the task facing you is merely inventory. That is a task similar to inventorying what clothes you've got in your closet, before you decide which ones to give away. Only, here, the closet is your head, and you're inventorying all the stuff that's in *there.* Don't try to evaluate your degree of mastery of a particular subject. Put down something you've only read a few articles about (*if it interests you*) side by side with a subject you studied for three semesters in school.

Throwaway comes later (*though, obviously, if there's a subject you hate so much you can barely stand to write it down, then . . . don't . . . write . . . it . . . down*).

When filling out this chart, do not forget to list those things you've learned–no matter how– about Organizations (including volunteer organizations), and what it takes to make them work.

It is not necessary that you should have ever taken a course in management or business. As the late John Crystal used to say, "Who cares how you learned it, whether in school or by sitting on the end of a log?" Examples of things you may know something about (and should list here) are: accounting or bookkeeping; administration; applications; computer programming, credit collection of overdue bills; customer relations and service; data analysis; distribution; fiscal analysis; government contracts; group dynamics or work with groups in general; hiring, human resources, or manpower; international business; management; marketing, sales; merchandising; packaging; performance specifications; planning; policy development; problem solving or other types of troubleshooting with operations or management systems; production; public speaking/addressing people; R & D program management; recruiting; show or conference planning, organization, and management; systems analysis; travel or travel planning, especially international travel; etc.

The Subjects Chart

SUBJECTS I KNOW SOMETHING ABOUT

Which column you decide to put a subject in, below, doesn't matter at all. The columns are only a series of pegs, to hang your memories on. Which peg is of no concern. Jot down a subject anywhere you like.

Column 1	Column 2	Column 3	Column 4	Column 5
Studied in High School or College or Graduate School	Learned on the Job	Learned from Conferences, Workshops, Training, Seminars	Learned at Home: Reading, TV, Tape Programs, Study Courses	Learned in My Leisure Time: Volunteer Work, Hobbies, etc.
Examples: *Spanish, Typing, Accounting, Computer Literacy, Psychology, Geography*	Examples: *Publishing, Computer Graphics, How an Organization Works, How to Operate Various Machines*	Examples: *Welfare Rules, Job-hunting, Painting, Utilizing the Internet*	Examples: *Art Appreciation, History, Speed Reading, A Language*	Examples: *Landscaping, How to Sew, Antiques, Camping, Stamps*

PRIORITIZING "THE SUBJECTS CHART"

When you're done, you may want to tape this Chart up on your refrigerator door for a few days, while you see if there's anything you want to add.

But when you're sure you've listed all you want to on the chart, it is crucial then to sort and then prioritize all these Fields, using the Prioritizing Grids on the following pages.

When you've got your ten prioritized Fields, then go on to the next item.

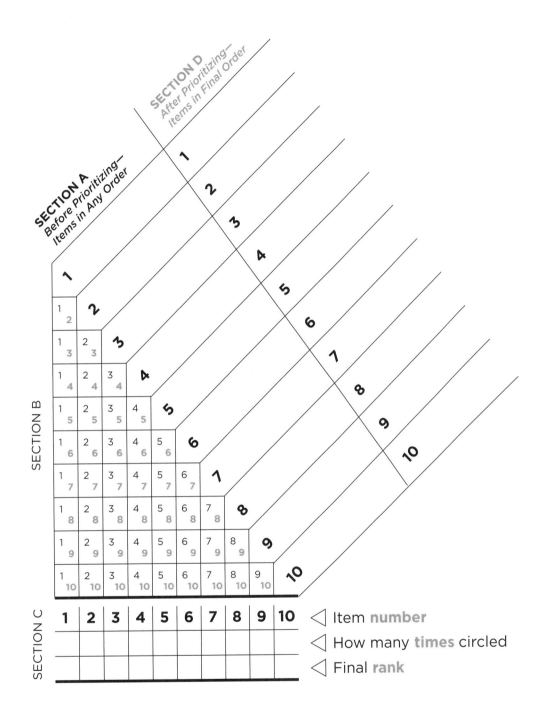

PRIORITIZING GRID FOR 10 ITEMS

```
1  1  1  1  1  1  1  1  1  1  1  1  1  1  1  1  1  1  1  1  1  1  1
   2  3  4  5  6  7  8  9  10 11 12 13 14 15 16 17 18 19 20 21 22 23 24

2  2  2  2  2  2  2  2  2  2  2  2  2  2  2  2  2  2  2  2  2  2  2
   3  4  5  6  7  8  9  10 11 12 13 14 15 16 17 18 19 20 21 22 23 24

3  3  3  3  3  3  3  3  3  3  3  3  3  3  3  3  3  3  3  3  3  3
   4  5  6  7  8  9  10 11 12 13 14 15 16 17 18 19 20 21 22 23 24

4  4  4  4  4  4  4  4  4  4  4  4  4  4  4  4  4  4  4  4  4
   5  6  7  8  9  10 11 12 13 14 15 16 17 18 19 20 21 22 23 24

5  5  5  5  5  5  5  5  5  5  5  5  5  5  5  5  5  5  5  5
   6  7  8  9  10 11 12 13 14 15 16 17 18 19 20 21 22 23 24

6  6  6  6  6  6  6  6  6  6  6  6  6  6  6  6  6  6  6
   7  8  9  10 11 12 13 14 15 16 17 18 19 20 21 22 23 24

7  7  7  7  7  7  7  7  7  7  7  7  7  7  7  7  7  7
   8  9  10 11 12 13 14 15 16 17 18 19 20 21 22 23 24

8  8  8  8  8  8  8  8  8  8  8  8  8  8  8  8  8
   9  10 11 12 13 14 15 16 17 18 19 20 21 22 23 24

9  9  9  9  9  9  9  9  9  9  9  9  9  9  9  9
   10 11 12 13 14 15 16 17 18 19 20 21 22 23 24

10 10 10 10 10 10 10 10 10 10 10 10 10 10
   11 12 13 14 15 16 17 18 19 20 21 22 23 24

11 11 11 11 11 11 11 11 11 11 11 11 11
   12 13 14 15 16 17 18 19 20 21 22 23 24

12 12 12 12 12 12 12 12 12 12 12 12
   13 14 15 16 17 18 19 20 21 22 23 24

13 13 13 13 13 13 13 13 13 13 13
   14 15 16 17 18 19 20 21 22 23 24

14 14 14 14 14 14 14 14 14 14
   15 16 17 18 19 20 21 22 23 24

15 15 15 15 15 15 15 15 15
   16 17 18 19 20 21 22 23 24

16 16 16 16 16 16 16 16
   17 18 19 20 21 22 23 24

17 17 17 17 17 17 17
   18 19 20 21 22 23 24

18 18 18 18 18 18
   19 20 21 22 23 24

19 19 19 19 19
   20 21 22 23 24

20 20 20 20
   21 22 23 24

21 21 21
   22 23 24

22 22
   23 24

23
   24
```

Total times each number got circled.

1	2	3	4	5	6
7	8	9	10	11	12
13	14	15	16	17	18
19	20	21	22	23	24

OPTIONAL PRIORITIZING GRID FOR 24 ITEMS

2. Fields Dealing with People's Problems or Needs

The question here is: **if you like to help people, what problems or needs do you like to help them with?** Each of these is a field.

In order to answer this question, it is helpful to fill out either of two kinds of exercises: *A checklist*, or "*fill in the blank*." Better yet, the two together, *like this*:

 1 Check off any kind of need you think you *might* like to help people with, and then

2 Add *which part of it*, or *what aspect of it*, you find particularly interesting or *appealing*.

THE PEOPLE LIST

I'd like to help people with their need for:

❑ **Clothing** (people's need to find and choose appropriate and affordable clothing); *and in my case what interests me particularly is* _____
_____ .

❑ **Food** (people's need to be fed, to be saved from starvation or poor nutrition); *and in my case what interests me particularly is* _____
_____ .

❑ **Housing** and **real estate** (people's need to find appropriate and affordable housing, apartment, office, or land); *and in my case what interests me particularly is* _____
_____ .

❑ **Languages** (people's need for literacy, to be able to read, or to learn a new language); *and in my case what interests me particularly is* _____
_____ .

❑ **Personal services** or **service occupations** (people's need to have someone do tasks they can't do, or haven't time to do, or don't want to do, for themselves—ranging from child care to helping run a farm); *and in my case what interests me particularly is* _____
_____ .

❑ **Family and consumer economics** (people's need to have help with budgeting, taxes, financial planning, money management, etc.); *and in my case what interests me particularly is*
_____
_____ .

❑ **Retail sales** (people's need for help in buying something); *and in my case what interests me particularly is* _____
_____
_____ .

❑ **Automobile sales** (people's need for transportation); *and in my case what interests me particularly is* _____
_____ .

❑ **Legal services** (people's need for expert counseling concerning the legal implications of things they are doing, or things that have been done to them); *and in my case what interests me particularly is* _____
_____ .

❑ **Child development** (people's need for help with various problems as their children are moving from infancy through childhood, including behavioral disabilities); *and in my case what interests me particularly is* _____
_____ .

❑ **Physical fitness** (people's need to get their body in tune through physical or occupational therapy, bodywork, exercise, or diet); *and in my case what interests me particularly is* _____
_____ .

❑ **Health services** (people's need to have preventive medicine or help with ailments, allergies, and disease); *and in my case what interests me particularly is* _____
_____ .

❑ **Healing** including **alternative medicine** and **holistic health** (people's need to have various injuries, ailments, maladies, or diseases healed); *and in my case what interests me particularly is* _____
_____ .

❑ **Medicine** (people's need to have help with diagnosing, treating various diseases, or removing diseased or badly injured parts of their body, etc.); *and in my case what interests me particularly is* _____
_____ .

❑ **Mental health** (people's need for help with stress, depression, insomnia, or other forms of emotional or mental disturbance); *and in my case what interests me particularly is* _____
_____ .

❑ **Psychology** or **psychiatry** (people's need for help with mental illness); *and in my case what interests me particularly is* _____
_____ .

❑ **Personal counseling and guidance** (people's need for help with family relations, with dysfunctions, or with various crises in their life, including a lack of balance in their use of time); *and in my case what interests me particularly is* _____
_____
_____ .

❑ **Career counseling, career-change,** or **life/work planning** (people's need for help in choosing a career or planning a life that has meaning and purpose); *and in my case what interests me particularly is*
_____
_____ .

- ❑ **Job-hunting, job-placement,** or **vocational rehabilitation** (people's need to have help in finding the work they have chosen, particularly when handicapped, or unemployed, or enrolling for welfare); *and in my case what interests me particularly is*_____ _____ .

- ❑ **Training** or **learning** (people's need to learn more about something, at work or outside of work); *and in my case what interests me particularly is* _____ _____ .

- ❑ **Entertainment** (people's need to be entertained, by laughter, wit, intelligence, or beauty); *and in my case what interests me particularly is* _____ _____ .

- ❑ **Spirituality** or **religion** (people's need to learn as much as they can about God, character, and their own soul, including their values and principles); *and in my case what interests me particularly is* _____ _____ .

- ❑ **Animals** or **plants** (their need for nurturing, growth, health, and other life cycles that require the kinds of sensitivities often referred to as interpersonal skills); *and in my case what interests me particularly is*_____ _____ .

- ❑ Other fields (or people's needs) not listed above, or a new field I just invented (I think): _____ _____ _____ _____ _____ .

In each question where it says "*. . . and in my case what interests me particularly is . . .*" think whether there are particular age groups you prefer to work with, and a particular gender you prefer to work with, and whether you prefer to work with individuals or groups, people of a particular background or set of beliefs, or people in a particular place (the armed forces, government, prison, mental institutions, etc.). If so, write it in.

PRIORITIZING "THE PEOPLE LIST"

When you're done, you may want to let this List just sit on your refrigerator door for a few days, while you see if there's anything you want to add.

But when you're sure you've added all you want to the List, it is crucial then to sort and then prioritize these Fields, using our now familiar Prioritizing Grid (on the next page). Then go on to the next item.

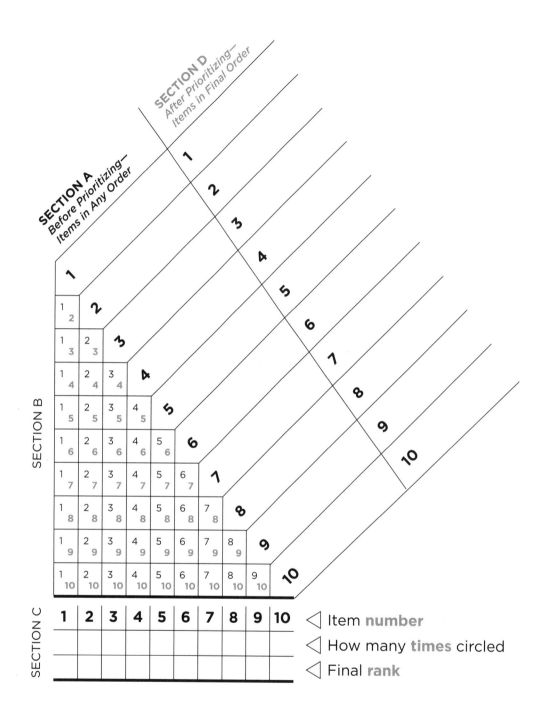

PRIORITIZING GRID FOR 10 ITEMS

3. Fields Dealing with Things, Tools, or Products

The question here is: **what things or products interest you the most?** (A product may be "a service," incidentally.)

Sampler: do you love to deal with, handle, construct, operate, market, or repair: *airplanes, antiques, bicycles, blueprints, books, bridges, clothing, computers, crops, diagrams, drugs, electricity, electronics, farm machinery, farms, fish, flowers, gardens, groceries, guidebooks, houses, kitchen appliances, lawns, machines, magazines, makeup, manuals, medicines, minerals, money, music, musical instruments, newspapers, office machines, paints, paper, plants, radios, rivers, rooms, sailboats, security systems, sewing machines, skiing equipment, soil, telephones, toiletries, tools, toys, trains, trees, valuable objects, videotapes, wine, wood—or what?*

What things or products do you *love* to deal with? In order to answer this question, you need to compile a *list*. And it is important that it is complete—that is, it's important that it list *all* the things or products that you love to deal with, in any way, shape, or form.

So, the brief *Sampler* above will not do. You need a longer list, and one that identifies which Fields those *things or products* are in. Fortunately, there is such a directory—at your very fingertips. It's called: the *yellow pages*, from your local telephone company. It has it all: things, products, fields, *and*—what you'll need later—the *location* of relevant organizations in your chosen geographical area.

The instructions for this exercise are simple. Go through the *table of contents* or *the index* of the yellow pages (in a phone book you don't mind marking up), and highlight any and every category or Field where you think you *might* like to deal with, or handle, or construct, or operate, or market, or repair *that thing, product, or service*. It is best to work your way backward, from Z to A. Then, go back, and looking only at the items you highlighted, circle in red the ones that you care the most about. Jot down their names on the next page.

If you don't plan to stay in your current community for this next job-hunt or career-change, then you will want to write to the phone company in the geographical area you are planning to move to, and secure their phone book. In the meantime, you can use your local phone directory for this exercise (just ignore locations). If a physical copy of either of those isn't available, see if there is an online version of same.

FLESHING OUT "THE THINGS PHONE BOOK"

When you're done, you may want to let this Phone Book exercise just sit on your refrigerator door for a few days, while you see if there's anything you want to add.

THE THINGS PHONE BOOK

_____   _____   _____   _____

_____   _____   _____   _____

_____   _____   _____   _____

_____   _____   _____   _____

_____   _____   _____   _____

_____   _____   _____   _____

_____   _____   _____   _____

_____   _____   _____   _____

_____   _____   _____   _____

_____   _____   _____   _____

_____   _____   _____   _____

_____   _____   _____   _____

_____   _____   _____   _____

_____   _____   _____   _____

Putting All Your Favorite Fields Together

And now that you're done with the three different skills lists—Subjects, People Problems, and Things—what have you got? You've got a prioritized list of your favorite Subjects, _and_ a prioritized list of your favorite People Problems, _and_ a kind of hodge-podge unprioritized list of your favorite Things, above. What you need to do at this point is put all three lists together, so as to make one list totaling ten items. Maybe pick the three top items from your Subjects list, and the three top items from your People Problems list, and any four from the Things list above, that you choose at random, on a hunch. Or any other proportion from the three lists that appeals to you. Just so you end up with ten fields, all told.

Then you need to take your ten items, and run them through the Grid on the next page. Your question, as you confront each pair: "If my job let me work at least part-time in this field, but not in this other one, and I had another job offer that let me work at least part-time in the other field, but not in the first, which job offer would I accept—other things being equal?" Once you're finished, and you have Section D all filled out, choose your top five (favorite fields) and copy them onto the Special Knowledges petal on page 2.

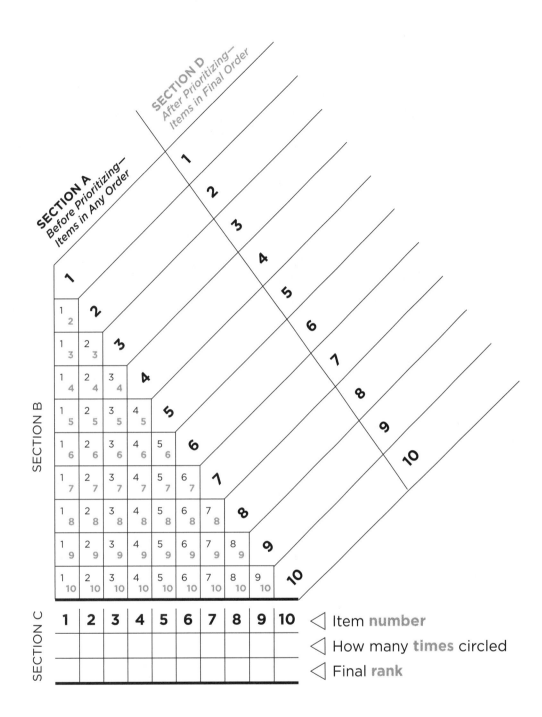

SECTION A
Before Prioritizing—
Items in Any Order

SECTION D
After Prioritizing—
Items in Final Order

SECTION B

SECTION C

◁ Item **number**

◁ How many **times** circled

◁ Final **rank**

PRIORITIZING GRID FOR 10 ITEMS

Petal #3: **Your Favorite People-Environments**

With the great emphasis upon the importance of the environment, in recent years, it has become increasingly realized that jobs are environments, too. The most important environmental factor always turns out to be people, because every job, except possibly that of a full-fledged hermit, surrounds us with people to one degree or another.

Indeed, many a good job has been ruined by the people one is surrounded by. Many a mundane job has been made delightful by the people one is surrounded by. Therefore, it is important to think out what kinds of people you want to be surrounded by.

Dr. John L. Holland offers the best description of people-environments. He says there are six principal ones:

 The **Realistic** People-Environment: filled with people who prefer activities involving "the explicit, ordered, or systematic manipulation of objects, tools, machines, and animals." "Realistic," incidentally, refers to Plato's conception of "the real" as that which one can apprehend through the senses.

I summarize this as: **R** = people who like nature, or athletics, or tools and machinery.

The **Investigative** People-Environment: filled with people who prefer activities involving "the observation and symbolic, systematic, creative investigation of physical, biological, or cultural phenomena."

I summarize this as: **I** = people who are very curious, and like to investigate or analyze data or people, or how things work.

The **Artistic** People-Environment: filled with people who prefer activities involving "ambiguous, free, unsystematized activities and competencies to create art forms or products."

I summarize this as: **A** = people who are very artistic, imaginative, and creative.

4 The **Social** People-Environment: filled with people who prefer activities involving "the manipulation of others to inform, train, develop, cure, or enlighten."

I summarize this as: **S** = people who are bent on trying to help, teach, or serve people.

5 The **Enterprising** People-Environment: filled with people who prefer activities involving "the manipulation of others to attain organizational or self-interest goals."

I summarize this as: **E** = people who like to start up projects or organizations, and/or be "up front" so as to entertain, influence, persuade, or sell to people.

6 The **Conventional** People-Environment: filled with people who prefer activities involving "the explicit, ordered, systematic manipulation of data, such as keeping records, filing materials, reproducing materials, organizing written and numerical data according to a prescribed plan, and operating business and data-processing machines."

I summarize this as: **C** = people who like detailed work, and like to complete tasks or projects.

According to John's theory and findings, everyone has three preferred people-environments, from among these six. The letters for your three preferred people-environments give you what is called your "Holland Code."

> There is, incidentally, a relationship between the people you like to be surrounded by *and* your skills *and* your values. See John Holland's book, *Making Vocational Choices* (3rd ed., 1997). You can procure it by going to the Psychological Assessment Resources website at www3.parinc.com or calling 1-800-331-8378. The book is $52.00 at this writing. PAR also has John Holland's instrument, called *The Self-Directed Search* (or SDS, for short), for discovering what your Holland Code is. PAR lets you take the test online for a small fee ($4.95) at www.self-directed-search.com.

I invented, many years ago, a quick and easy way to obtain your Holland Code (it has a 93 percent correspondence with Holland's Self-Directed Search). I call it the Party Exercise. In case you want to do it, here's how the exercise goes.

On the next page is an aerial view of a room in which a party is taking place. At this party, people with the same or similar interests have (for some reason) all gathered in the same corner of the room.

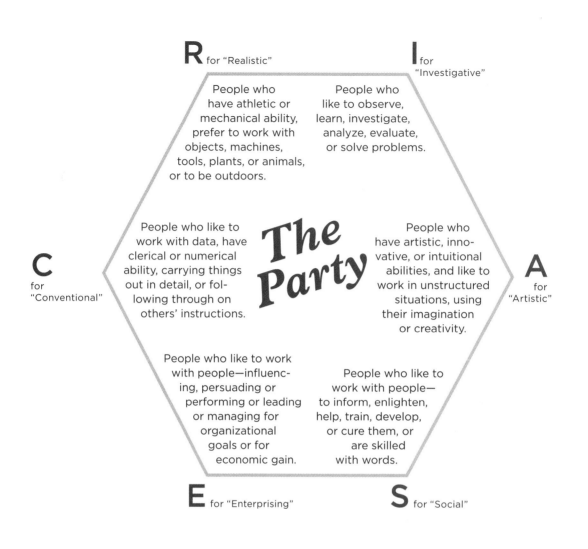

R for "Realistic"

People who have athletic or mechanical ability, prefer to work with objects, machines, tools, plants, or animals, or to be outdoors.

I for "Investigative"

People who like to observe, learn, investigate, analyze, evaluate, or solve problems.

C for "Conventional"

People who like to work with data, have clerical or numerical ability, carrying things out in detail, or following through on others' instructions.

The Party

A for "Artistic"

People who have artistic, innovative, or intuitional abilities, and like to work in unstructured situations, using their imagination or creativity.

E for "Enterprising"

People who like to work with people—influencing, persuading or performing or leading or managing for organizational goals or for economic gain.

S for "Social"

People who like to work with people—to inform, enlighten, help, train, develop, or cure them, or are skilled with words.

 1 Which corner of the room would you instinctively be drawn to, as the group of people you would most enjoy being with for the longest time? (Leave aside any question of shyness, or whether you would have to talk to them.) Write the letter for that corner here:

2 After fifteen minutes, everyone in the corner you have chosen leaves for another party crosstown, except you. Of the groups that still remain now, which corner or group would you be drawn to the most, as the people you would most enjoy being with for the longest time? Write the letter for that corner here:

3 After fifteen minutes, this group also leaves for another party, except you. Of the corners, and groups, which remain now, which one would you most enjoy being with for the longest time? Write the letter for that corner here:

The three letters you just chose, in the three steps, are called your "Holland Code." Here is what you should now do:

 1 **Circle them on the People-Environments petal, on page 3.**

Put three circles around your favorite corner; two circles around your next favorite; and one circle around your third favorite.

2 **Once the corners are circled, you may wish to write up (for yourself and your eyes only) a temporary statement about your future job or career, using the descriptors above.**

If your "Code" turned out to be IAS, for example, you might write:
"I would like a job or career best if I was surrounded by people who are very curious, and like to investigate or analyze things (I); who are also very innovative (A); and who are bent on trying to help or serve people (S)."

3 **Finally, here, look over the skills you have just described in *others*, and see how much of this is also true of you.**

What I call "The Mirror Theory" holds that we often see *ourselves* best by looking into the faces of others. Hence, once we have described the people we would most like to be surrounded by, in many cases we have also described ourselves. ("Birds of a feather flock together.") So, look over the circled items on your People-Environments petal. Are these, perchance, *your* favorite proclivities, skills, tasks, etc.? Or not?

Petal #4: **Your Favorite Working Conditions**

Plants that grow beautifully at sea level often perish if they're taken ten thousand feet up the mountain. Likewise, we do our best work under certain conditions, but not under others. Thus, the question: What are your favorite "working conditions"? actually is a question about "Under what circumstances do you do your most effective work?"

The best way to approach this is by starting with the things you disliked in any of your previous jobs, using the chart on the next page to list these. You may copy this chart onto a larger piece of paper if you wish, before you begin filling it out. When you get to Column A, begin with such factors as: "too noisy," "too much supervision," "no windows in my workplace," "having to be at work by 6 a.m.," etc.

When you get to Column B, you must rank these factors that are in Column A, in their exact order of importance, to you. As always, if you are baffled as to how to prioritize these factors in exact order, use the Prioritizing Grid that follows. The question to ask yourself, there, as you confront each "pair" is: "If I were offered two jobs, and in the first job I would be rid of this first distasteful working condition, but not the second, while in the second job, I would be rid of the second distasteful working condition, but not the first, which distasteful working condition would I choose to get rid of?"

Note that when you later come to Column C, and list the "positive" form of the factors in Column B, your positive factors will already be prioritized: that is, the opposite of the thing you hated the most in the past becomes the condition you feel is the most important for you to find, in the future. Note that the "positive" form of the factor is not necessarily its direct opposite: "too much supervision" in Column B may become "a moderate amount of supervision on a weekly or semi-weekly basis" in Column C.

Once you've finished Column C, enter the top five factors from there on the Working Conditions petal of the Flower Diagram, on page 3.

DISTASTEFUL WORKING CONDITIONS

	Column A — Distasteful Working Conditions	Column B — Distasteful Working Conditions Ranked	Column C + The Keys to My Effectiveness at Work
Places I Have Worked Thus Far in My Life	*I Have Learned from the Past That My Effectiveness at Work Is Decreased When I Have to Work Under These Conditions:*	*I Have Run the Factors in Column A Through the Prioritizing Grid on the Next Page, and Here Is My Ranking from Section D there, beginning with the factor I dislike (or even hate) the most from my past jobs:*	*Here is the positive form of the factors in Column B, in order:*
		1.	1.
		2.	2.
		3.	3.
		4.	4.
		5.	5.
		6.	6.
		7.	7.
		8.	8.
		9.	9.
		10.	10.
			I Believe My Effectiveness Would Be at an Absolute Maximum, If I Could Work Under These Conditions

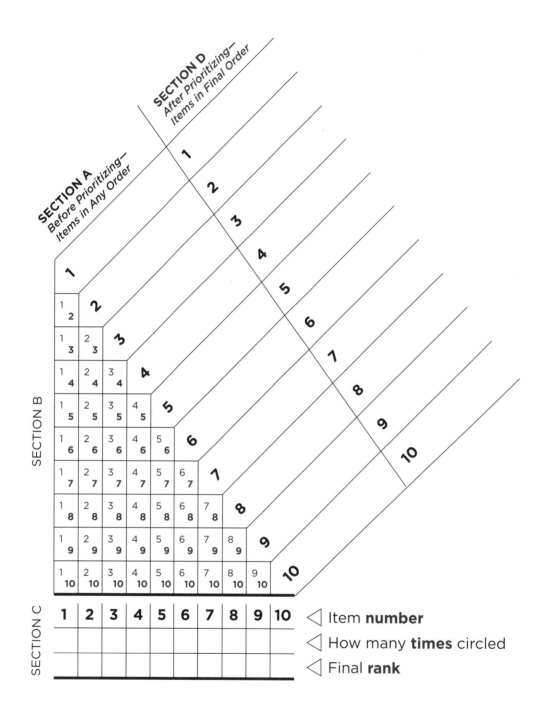

PRIORITIZING GRID FOR 10 ITEMS

Petal #5: **Level of Responsibility and Salary**

Salary is something you must think out ahead of time, when you're contemplating your ideal job or career. Level goes hand in hand with salary, of course.

1. The first question here is, at what level would you like to work, in your ideal job?

Level is a matter of how much responsibility you want in an organization:

- ❏ Boss or CEO (this may mean you'll have to form your own business)
- ❏ Manager or someone under the boss who carries out orders, but also gives them
- ❏ The head of a team
- ❏ A member of a team of equals

- ❏ One who works in tandem with one other partner
- ❏ One who works alone, either as an employee or as a consultant to an organization, or as a one-person business

Enter a two- or three-word summary of your answer, on the Level of Responsibility and Salary petal of the Flower Diagram, on page 3.

2. The second question here is, what salary would you like to be aiming for?

Here you have to think in terms of minimum or maximum. Minimum is what you would need to make if you were just barely "getting by." And you need to know this *before* you go in for a job interview with anyone (*or before you form your own business, where you'll have to know ahead of time how much profit you must make, just to survive*).

Maximum could be any astronomical figure you can think of, but it is more useful here to put down the salary you realistically think you could make, with your present competency and experience, were you working for a real, *but generous*, boss. (If this maximum figure is still depressingly low, then put down the salary you would like to be making five years from now.)

Make out a detailed outline of your estimated expenses *now*, listing what you need *monthly* in the following categories:[3]

Housing

Rent or mortgage payments . . . . $ _____

Electricity/gas. . . . . $ _____

Water . . . . $ _____

Telephone. . . . . $ _____

Garbage removal. . . . . $ _____

Cleaning, maintenance, repairs[4] . . . . $ _____

Food

What you spend at the supermarket

and/or farmer's market, etc. . . . . $ _____

Eating out. . . . . $ _____

Clothing

Purchase of new or used clothing . . . . $ _____

Cleaning, dry cleaning, laundry . . . . $ _____

Automobile/transportation[5]

Car payments . . . . $ _____

Gas. . . . . $ _____

Repairs . . . . $ _____

Public transportation (*bus, train, plane*). . . . . $ _____

3. If this kind of financial figuring is not your cup of tea, find a buddy, friend, relative, family member, or anyone, who can help you do this. If you don't know anyone who could do this, go to your local church, synagogue, religious center, social club, gym, or wherever you hang out, and ask the leader or manager there, to help you find someone. If there's a bulletin board, put up a notice on the bulletin board. You can also try online budgeting calculators at websites like Mint.com or Yahoo!Finance.

4. If you have extra household expenses, such as a security system, be sure to include the quarterly (or whatever) expenses here, divided by three.

5. Your checkbook stubs will tell you a lot of this stuff. But you may be vague about your cash or credit card expenditures. For example, you may not know how much you spend on gas, or how much you spend at the supermarket, etc. But there is a simple way to find out. Just carry a little notepad and pen around with you for two weeks or more, and jot down everything you pay cash (or use credit cards) for—on the spot, right after you pay it. At the end of those two weeks, you'll be able to take that notepad and make a realistic guess of what should be put down in these categories that now puzzle you. (Multiply the two-weeks figure by two, and you'll have the monthly figure.) You can also check your credit or debit card statements through online banking.

6. Incidentally, for U.S. citizens, looking ahead to next April 15, be sure to check with your local IRS office or a reputable accountant to find out if you can deduct the expenses of your job-hunt on your federal (and state) income tax returns. At this writing, some job-hunters can, if—big IF—this is not your first job that you're looking for, if you haven't been unemployed too long, and if you aren't making a career-change. Do go find out what the latest "ifs" are. If the IRS tells you you are eligible, keep careful receipts of everything related to your job-hunt, as you go along: telephone calls, stationery, printing, postage, travel, etc.

Insurance

    Car . . . . $ _____

    Medical or health care . . . . $ _____

    House and personal possessions . . . . $ _____

    Life . . . . $ _____

Medical expenses

    Doctors' visits . . . . $ _____

    Prescriptions . . . . $ _____

    Fitness costs . . . . $ _____

Support for other family members

    Child-care costs (*if you have children*) . . . . $ _____

    Child support (*if you're paying that*) . . . . $ _____

    Support for your parents (*if you're helping out*) . . . . $ _____

Charity giving/tithe (*to help others*) . . . . $ _____

School/learning

    Children's costs (*if you have children in school*) . . . . $ _____

    Your learning costs (*adult education, job-hunting classes, etc.*) . . . . $ _____

Pet care (*if you have pets*) . . . . $ _____

Bills and debts (*usual monthly payments*)

    Credit cards . . . . $ _____

    Student loans . . . . $ _____

    Other obligations you pay off monthly . . . . $ _____

Taxes

    Federal[6] (*next April's due, divided by months remaining until then*) . . . . $ _____

    State (*likewise*) . . . . $ _____

    Local/property (*next amount due, divided by*

    months remaining until then) . . . . $ _____

    Tax-help (*if you ever use an accountant,*

    pay a friend to help you with taxes, etc.) . . . . $ _____

Savings . . . . $ _____

Retirement (Keogh, IRA, Sep, etc.) . . . . $ _____

Amusement/discretionary spending

    Movies, DVD rentals, Netflix subscription, etc. . . . . $ _____

    Other kinds of entertainment . . . . $ _____

    Reading, newspapers, magazines, books . . . . $ _____

    Gifts (*birthday, holidays, etc.*) . . . . $ _____

    Vacations . . . . $ _____

Total Amount You Need Each Month . . . . $ _____

Multiply the total amount you need each month by 12 to get the yearly figure. Divide the yearly figure by 2,000, and you will be reasonably near the minimum hourly wage that you need. Thus, if you need $3,333 per month, multiplied by 12 that's $40,000 a year, and then divided by 2,000, that's $20 an hour.

Parenthetically, you may want to prepare two different versions of the above budget: **one** with the expenses you'd ideally *like* to make, and **the other** a minimum budget, which will give you what you are looking for, here: the floor, below which you simply cannot afford to go.

Enter the maximum, and minimum, on your Level of Responsibility and Salary petal on the Flower Diagram on page 3.

Optional Exercise: You may wish to put down other rewards, besides money, that you would hope for, from your next job or career. These might be:

- ❏ Adventure
- ❏ Challenge
- ❏ Respect
- ❏ Influence
- ❏ Popularity
- ❏ Fame
- ❏ Power
- ❏ Intellectual stimulation from the other workers there

- ❏ A chance to exercise leadership
- ❏ A chance to be creative
- ❏ A chance to make decisions
- ❏ A chance to use my expertise
- ❏ A chance to help others
- ❏ A chance to bring others closer to God or spirituality
- ❏ Other: _____

If you do check off things on this list, arrange your answers in order of importance to you, and then add them to the Level of Responsibility and Salary petal on page 3.

Petal #6: **Geography**

Even if you love where you are now, or even if you're stuck where you are now, you never know when an opportunity may suddenly open up for you, down the road. You want to be ready. Don't wait until then to do this exercise; do it now!

The question you need to answer is: **Where would you most like to live and work, if you had a choice (besides where you are now)?** In answering this question, it is important—before you come to names—to list the geographical factors that are important to you.

To help you do this, fill out the chart on pages 54–55. *(You may copy it onto a larger piece of paper if you wish, before you begin working on it. And, if you are doing this exercise with a partner, make a copy of the chart for them also before you start filling it out, so that each of you may have a "clean" copy of your own.)* Follow the instructions starting on page 56.

MY GEOGRAPHICAL PREFERENCES
Decision Making for Just You

Column 1 Names of Places I Have Lived	Column 2 From the Past: Negatives	Column 3 Translating the Negatives into Positives	Column 4 Ranking of My Positives
	Factors I Disliked and Still Dislike about Any Place		1.
	1.	1.	2.
	2.	2.	
	3.	3.	3.
	4.	4.	4.
	5.	5.	
	6.	6.	5.
	7.	7.	6.
	8.	8.	
	9.	9.	7.
	10.	10.	
		Other Factors I Liked, Always Liked, About One of Those Places	8.
			9.
			10.

OUR GEOGRAPHICAL PREFERENCES
Decision Making for You and a Partner

Column 5 Places Suggested to Me That Fit the Criteria in Column 4	Column 6 Ranking of His/Her Preferences	Column 7 Combining Our Two Lists (Columns 4 & 6)	Column 8 Places That Fit These Criteria
(If You Are Doing This Exercise with a Partner, You Will Not Need to Fill in This Column; as Column 8 Replaces It. Proceed Now with Your Partner to Column 6.)	a.	a.	
		1.	
	b.	b.	
		2.	
	c.	c.	
		3.	
	d.	d.	
		4.	
	e.	e.	
		5.	
		Optional:	
	f.	*f.*	
		6.	
	g.	*g.*	
		7.	
	h.	*h.*	
		8.	
	i.	*i.*	
		9.	
	j.	*j.*	
		10.	

This is how you fill out the chart. There are seven easy steps:

 List all the places (towns, cities, etc.) where you have ever lived. These go in Column 1.

 List the factors you disliked and still dislike about each place. Naturally, there will be some repetition. In which case, just put an extra check mark in front of any factor you have already written down, when it comes up again. All of these negative factors go in Column 2.

 Then take each of those negative factors and translate the negatives into positives. This will not *necessarily* be the opposite. For example, "rains all the time" does not necessarily translate into "sunny all the time." It might be more like: "sunny at least 200 days a year." *It's your call.* All these positive factors go in Column 3. Feel free to add at the bottom of the column here any positive factors you remember, off the top of your head, about the places in Column 1.

 Now, rank your positive factors list (Column 3) in their order of importance, to you. They will be things like: "has cultural opportunities," "skiing in the winter," "good newspaper," etc. After using this Grid on the opposite page, list in Column 4 your top ten positive factors, as they appeared in Section D of the Grid. If you are baffled as to how to decide between each element here in the Grid, the question to ask yourself as you confront each "pair" is: "If I could live in a place that had this first factor, but not the second, or if I could live in another place that had the second factor, but not the first, in which place would I choose to live?"

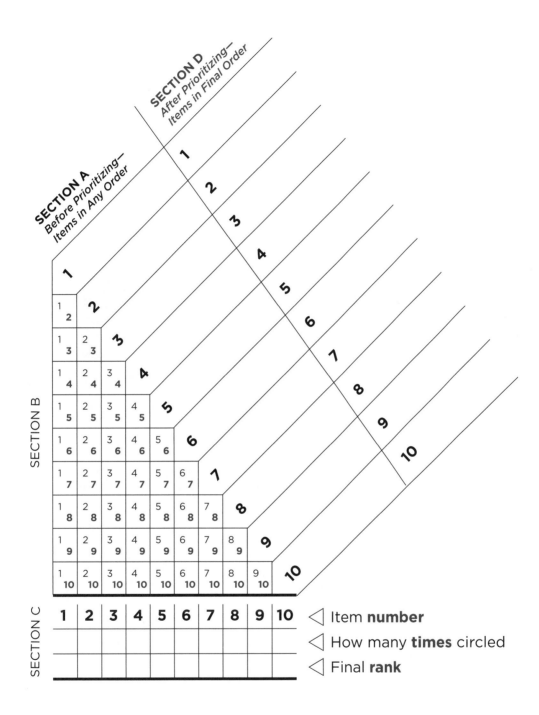

SECTION A
*Before Prioritizing—
Items in Any Order*

SECTION D
*After Prioritizing—
Items in Final Order*

SECTION B

SECTION C

◁ Item **number**

◁ How many **times** circled

◁ Final **rank**

PRIORITIZING GRID FOR 10 ITEMS

5 **When you are done, show this list of ten prioritized, positive factors to everyone you know, and ask them what cities, towns, or places they know of that have all or most of these factors.** You want to particularly emphasize the top factors, the ones that are the most important to you. If there is only a partial overlap between your factors and the places your friends suggest, make sure the overlap is in the factors you placed first on your list.

6 **From all the names your friends suggest to you, choose the three that look most intriguing to you, in order of your personal preference, based on what you now know.** These go in Column 5. These are the places you will want to find out more about, until you are sure which is your absolute first preference, second, and third.

7 **Now, go back to the Flower Diagram on pages 2–3, and copy the place names from Column 5 (or 8) onto the Geography petal.** You are done with geography. You now know the place(s) to find out more about, through their Chamber of Commerce, the Internet, a summer visit, etc.

If you are doing this with a partner, you will not use Column 5. Instead, copy *their* Column 4 into your Column 6. Then alternately combine *their* first five factors and *your* first five factors, until you wind up with a list of ten altogether. (First you list their top one, then your top one, then their second preference, then your second preference, etc.) This goes in Column 7. It is *this* list of ten positive factors that you both then show to *everyone* you know, to ask them what cities, towns, or places they know of that have all or most of these factors, *beginning with the top ones.* From all the names those friends suggest to you, you then choose the three places that look the most intriguing to both of you, and rank them in order. These go in Column 8.

Done!

Voilà! At last, if you've hung in all the way, your Flower Diagram should be complete. You will now have one of two reactions as you look over your Flower.

A Lightbulb Goes On

For some of you there will be a big *Aha!* as you look at your Flower Diagram. A lightbulb will go on, over your head, and you will say, "My goodness, I see *exactly* what sort of career this points me to." This happens particularly with intuitive people.

If you are one of those intuitive people, I say, "Good for you!" Just two gentle warnings, if I may: Don't prematurely close out *other* possibilities.

And *don't* say to yourself: "Well, I see what it is that I would die to be able to do, but I *know* there is no job in the world like that, that *I* would be able to get." Dear friend, you don't know any such thing. You haven't done your research yet. Of course, it is always possible that when you've completed all that research, and conducted your search, you still may not be able to find *all* that you want—down to the last detail. But you'd be surprised at how much of your dream you may be able to find.

Other Possibility, You Look at Your Flower Diagram and . . . a Lightbulb *Doesn't* Go On

In contrast to what I just said, many of you will look at your completed Flower Diagram, and you won't have *a clue* as to what job or career it points to. Soooo, we need a "fallback" strategy.

First, write down on one piece of paper your top five skills and your top four special knowledges from your Flower, and then ask at least five friends, family members, and professionals you know what job-titles and job-fields come to mind. Then, approach contacts in that field for Informational Interviews. During Informational Interviewing, you want to talk to people who are actually doing the work you think you'd love to do. Why? In effect, you are mentally *trying on jobs* to see if they fit you.

Once you discover places you'd like to work for, do some preliminary research on them before you approach them for an interview.

And remember, always send a thank-you note to anyone who helps you along the way.

Need More Help?

This should get you started toward finding your dream job, with the Flower as your guide. For more information on job-hunting, I invite you to consult with the book for which this workbook is a companion: *What Color Is Your Parachute? A Practical Manual for Job-Hunters and Career-Changers*, by yours truly.

Don't just drop your Flower at this point. Be persistent, be thorough, and don't give up just because your Flower doesn't immediately point you toward the next step. Keep showing your Flower to anyone and everyone, and ask what suggestions they can make. This is your life you're working on, your *Life*. Make it glorious.

About the Author

RICHARD N. BOLLES (often known by his familiar name, Dick Bolles) is widely acknowledged as the founder of the modern career development field, due to his writings for the past forty years. A member of Mensa and the Society for Human Resource Management, he has been the keynote speaker at hundreds of conferences. Bolles was trained in chemical engineering at Massachusetts Institute of Technology, and holds a bachelor's degree cum laude in physics from Harvard University, a master's in sacred theology from General Theological (Episcopal) Seminary in New York City, and three honorary doctorates. He lives in the San Francisco Bay Area with his wife, Marci.

Also by Richard N. Bolles

What Color Is Your Parachute?
A Practical Manual for Job-Hunters
and Career-Changers
10,000,000 COPIES SOLD
$18.99 paper (Canada: $20.99)
6 x 9 inches, 368 pages
ISBN 978-1-58008-270-9

The Job-Hunter's Survival Guide
How to Find Hope and Rewarding Work,
Even When "There Are No Jobs"
$9.99 paper (Canada: $12.99)
5 x 8 inches, 112 pages
ISBN 978-1-58008-026-2

Available from Ten Speed Press wherever books are sold.
www.tenspeed.com